Unusual Sayings

for

Usual Days

Readings for
Amusement and Action

Rodney Charles Dutton

R. C. Dutton Books

Dedicated to those who usually say unusual sayings on usual days

#1

Corpses are proof that you can be silent, and still not be a good listener.

Really good listeners are hard to find. Don't give people a stiff ear. Listen twice as much as you speak.

#2

Feelings are important, but most decisions cannot be based upon emotions. I'm sorry, but that's just how I feel.

Take a gift to a friend who is feeling down. Sit with them—talk a little, and listen a lot.

#3

People say, "Grown men don't cry." Tell them that while they're cutting onions.

Show compassion toward someone who is suffering.

#4

I'm lucky that I don't believe in luck.

Do something for someone that will make them feel fortunate.

#5

One of the difficulties with time travel is trying to find something in your closet for the time period you're going to visit.

Donate clothing you never wear to people who are in need.

#6

People's silence speaks volumes, but it's hard to know where to put the quotation marks.

Find an inspiring quote that will challenge you in your life.

#7

No one ever got carpal tunnel from having face-to-face conversations.

Stop texting for a moment and give your fingers a rest. Go see a friend; sit and talk with them. The effort given of driving to their house will make them feel valued.

#8

Some people eat fortune cookies to find a fortunate future. Others find themselves fortunate to just eat fortune cookies.

Take someone out to Chinese food.

#9

Life's a beach. This is the motto of all beach sand.

Take a trip to the beach with your family or friends.

#10

The sun and babies are alike—they both wake up early in the morning.

Wake up early and watch the sunrise.

From the rising of the sun to its setting, the name of the LORD is to be praised!

Psalm 113:3

#11

Hornless unicorns are easier to find than horned unicorns.

Go on a horseback ride with someone you love.

#12

Having the power of invisibility is great—until you need a hug.

Hug a family member or close friend, and tell them how much you appreciate them. Don't wait until they pass away, and disappear from your life on earth.

#13

If you had more legs, you could move as fast as a centipede does.

Go on a run, or take a walk. If you are not physically able to do that, then imagine yourself walking around your neighborhood. Please yield at the centipede crossings.

#14

The reason that Nailhead Sharks don't exist is because Hammerhead Sharks drove them into extinction.

Visit a local aquarium with a friend. Don't confuse swimming with the dolphins with swimming with the sharks.

#15

Birds have no arms. So, they just have to wing it.

Invite someone to go birding with you at a national park.

#16

Some people are like volcanoes; their hot temper erupts, spewing verbal burns all over the place.

Try repaying good for evil when someone speaks to you in anger.

Repay no one evil for evil, but give thought to do what is honorable in the sight of all. If possible, so far as it depends on you, live peaceably with all.

Romans 12:17-18

#17

Trees are somewhat like dogs. They stay in your backyard, bring you pleasure to watch, and shed all over the place.

Help an elderly person in your neighborhood rake the leaves in their yard.

#18

Getting rid of glitter is like fighting an incurable disease, no matter what you do, it spreads.

Send someone an encouraging greeting card you made yourself. (Glitter is optional.)

#19

No one can watch *all* of a movie or television show. You have to blink.

Go to the movies with your family or friends. The more of you there are, the less likely you are to all blink at the same moments. That way, they can fill in the parts you missed.

#20

Perseverance is a great trait to exhibit, except when you are literally beating your head against the wall.

Identify steps you can take to achieve one of your goals, and write them down. Don't give up despite difficulties or obstacles that may come your way.

#21

Too bad there are not speed bumps in the buffet line.

Start an exercise program, or increase the one you already follow.

#22

Procrastinators are just trying to advance the future. That's why their rallying cry is "*always tomorrow!*"

Finish a project you have been putting off for a long time.

#23

Death is the number-one killer in every nation. I was dying to tell you that.

Go visit someone who is terminally ill.

#24

Most things are better experienced in person. Pain may not be at the top of that list.

Be sensitive and caring toward those around you who are sick.

#25

Wild animals are those who roam free without I.D. collars, and have no human to pick up their poop.

Visit a wildlife sanctuary with someone who loves animals.

#26

Sunrise and sunset are two bookends, and between them the daily story of your life is written on the world.

Take advantage of the time you have on earth to make a difference. If your life was a book what kind would it be? A motivational essay, or an adventure story? An inspirational biography, or a story filled with drama?

#27

Dogs have a lot of traits we could stand to emulate. They are faithful, loyal, and always excited to see the people they are close to. Eating your own vomit is not one of the doggy-traits you should imitate.

Be a faithful and loyal friend, for these qualities always make friendships friendlier.

A friend loves at all times.

Proverbs 17:17

#28

If the ingredient list on your food is the length of a short novel, then you probably shouldn't be eating it.

Start eating healthily—your body will thank you. By consuming good food with a short ingredient list, you might find yourself with extra time on your hands. Use it to read real novels.

#29

Our lives would be a lot different if we welcomed and celebrated each new day as much as we celebrate the New Year.

Embrace and experience each new day with great joy. It's a gift we only have for twenty-four hours. Don't drop the ball on living each day to the fullest.

#30

Narcissistic Fibrosis is a condition in which a person talks excessively about themselves, their physical appearance, and their talents. As a result, their ongoing stream of superiority stifles the air around them, making it difficult for listeners to breathe.

Practice the virtue of humility.

Do nothing from rivalry or conceit, but in humility count others more significant than yourself.

Philippians 2:3

#31

Eviction is not another word for vacation, even though both of them involve leaving your house to go and spend time in a new place.

Take a relaxing vacation with family, or friends. Make sure you pay your rent before you leave.

#32

Selfishness is where you fish only for yourself, not sharing any of the fish you catch with others.

Share some of the excess of your possessions with the poor in your community.

#33

Sometimes when you love your enemy, you will find that you are loving yourself.

Make good and wise choices in your life. Don't become an enemy to yourself by choosing evil.

#34

A bookie is like a librarian. They both oversee books, advise their patrons on the due dates of their obligations, and fine them when they are delinquent.

Go to a library, enjoy the silence, and read a book.

#35

I Don't Know must be the most popular restaurant of all time. Quite the majority of people name this place when you ask them where they want to eat.

Take a person on a limited income out to eat at a nice restaurant.

#36

The world's countries are like selections in an ice cream parlor—they are all ice cream, but each one has its own unique flavor.

Eat ice cream while you plan a trip to a foreign country with an adventurous friend.

#37

For some people being a resident in a cemetery is the same as when they were a resident in a nursing home. No one comes to see them.

Go visit someone in a nursing home; they are waiting for a visit.

#38

Beach sand tells you to slow down; hour-glass sand tells you to speed up.

Spend an hour doing something that has an upcoming deadline.

#39

Film developers always dress modestly, but might be a little out-of-touch with world events. Yes, they never overexpose, and are in the dark a lot.

Print some of your favorite digital family photos. Frame and hang them in a prominent place to remind you of your memories together.

#40

Just because your house is green doesn't mean your plants will grow well.

Plant some flowers in an area where you can sit and enjoy them.

#41

People on airplanes get mad faster than people at sea level, because the boiling point at higher altitudes is lower.

Invite a friend over, boil some water, and have a tea party.

#42

If rivers were motionless, and land flowed, then I could sit in a canoe, stationary on the river, and watch the flowing hills, cascading down toward a sea of grass.

Take a canoe trip down a river, and watch the land pass by.

#43

Putting a mannequin in the front seat of your car so you can commute to work in the high occupancy lane is not wise. Mannequins are not good drivers. Why do you think we have the term *crash dummies*?

Be a courteous driver. There are already enough insensitive dummies out there behind the wheel.

#44

Car manufacturers should install a cup holder on the roof of their vehicles for when you forget your coffee cup up there. That way, you still have a chance of saving your coffee.

Go to a coffee shop and enjoy warm conversation with a friend over a hot cup of coffee.

#45

When I read a menu, I like one with a happy ending.

Many books have happy endings. The Bible has the happiest ending of all.

Therefore, if anyone is in Christ, he is a new creation. The old has passed away; behold, the new has come.

2 Corinthians 5:17

#46

A cup of hot non-caloric soup is the same as saying a cup of hot water.

Volunteer at a soup kitchen, and have a souper day.

#47

Going to a restaurant with a friend to talk and eat is better than doing so by yourself. That way, people won't think you're crazy for speaking to an empty chair.

Go to a restaurant with a friend to share a meal and some good conversation. Practice the art of listening more, and speaking less.

#48

If you plant tomato seeds, tomatoes will grow. If you plant apple seeds, apples will grow. If you plant bird seed, birds won't be able to eat it and grow, because you buried it.

Put some bird seed out for your neighborhood feathered friends.

#49

If you have to appear in court, make sure you dress well—wear a law suit.

Dress up and go out to eat at a nice restaurant with your spouse, or significant other. Leave your law suit at home in your closet.

#50

A common side effect of time travel is losing track of the days when you return to your own time. Many people refer to this as time machine lag.

When people are extremely late, or forget altogether about their appointment with you, show them mercy. They may have been doing a lot of time traveling lately.

#51

Love is a two-way street. As you become more serious in a relationship, look both ways before you cross the street to the other side in marriage. Your boyfriend's or girlfriend's ex may be driving toward you at high speed.

Accept the one you are going to marry as they are now, for they may never change. Choose to love, honor, and cherish them no matter what happens. Faithfulness to each other is not a luxury, it is essential.

#52

Selective Mirage Syndrome is where people in the desert see what they *want* to see of the things that are not really there.

Take a nature walk and observe all the things around you, big and small.

#53

Petroglyph is another way to say *outdoor prehistoric art museum.*

Write a poem or story about an experience you have had, and give the manuscript to your relatives. Paper will be easier to pass along to your descendants, than huge boulders.

#54

If we trained dogs to be postal carriers, then instead of biting those who deliver the mail, they could bite all the people they deliver the mail to.

Leave a note of thanks in your mailbox for your postal carrier's faithful service. He or she's job is not easy, and at the end of the day they are one tired puppy.

#55

During celebrations people break things. Like piñatas at birthdays, champagne bottles at ship christenings, and plate smashing at Greek weddings. Too bad our mothers are not celebratory when we accidentally break their things.

Tell your mother you love her, and that you're grateful for her patience.

#56

An elevator operator's life is full of ups and downs, but they daily embrace the privilege of lifting up people's lives.

You may be going through a difficult time, but try saying some encouraging words to those around you. In the midst of this action your spirits will be lifted up a little, and others will be encouraged.

#57

Our past should not be a pastime for us. If our past is our pastime, then we cannot enjoy the gift of today.

Forgive someone in your heart who has hurt you in the past.

Put on then, as God's chosen ones, holy and beloved, compassionate hearts, kindness, humility, meekness, and patience, bearing with one another and, if one has a complaint against another, forgiving each other; as the Lord has forgiven you, so you must also forgive. And above all these put on love, which binds everything together in perfect harmony. And let the peace of Christ rule in your hearts, to which indeed you were called in one body. And be thankful.

Colossians 3:12-15

#58

Oxygen is something we inhale but don't exhale. That sounds a lot like self-focused people who daily want to receive compliments, but never give them.

Make it a habit to daily compliment those around you who are doing good things.

#59

The word "dad" is a palindrome- its spelled the same forward and backward. If you mix up the order of the letters, it spells add. That makes sense because a person who lives up to the name *dad* adds good things to your life, and you can count on them from beginning to end.

Do something nice for your dad to show how much you love him, and that you appreciate all he has done for you.

#60

Siblings are those whom you frequently fight with, and always fight for.

Get your siblings together for a lengthy meal, and enjoyable conversation. Don't fight over the last serving of food.

#61

License plates are good when you are hungry for a drive to the park. Paper plates are good when you are hungry for food in the park.

Take a scenic drive to a park, and have a picnic with people you love. If you like, you can bring out the good china for this meal.

#62

Slot machines are like toilets. You pull the handle, and everything you put into it is sucked away.

Instead of going on a vacation to Las Vegas, and giving your money to the casinos, take a trip to some place new, and give your time volunteering at a charity organization.

#63

People frequently ask where the complaint box is when there is a problem. People rarely ask where the compliment box is when they receive good service.

Thank those who provide good service to you. It's time to start thinking outside the complaint box.

#64

Paper plates, paper bowls, paper cups, paper towels, paper napkins—these words are another way to say picnic litter. Remember the world is not your trash can. That kind of thinking is a bunch of rubbish. Put a lid on litter.

Volunteer to pick up trash in your community.

#65

Relationships come at a price. Some of them you may be struggling to break even on, while others may have ended in relational bankruptcy. Be thankful you have some good relationships you can bank on.

Do something to strengthen one of your relationships.

#66

You would think there would be a significant drop in gym memberships since so many people have become college graduates—they must get plenty of exercise at work trying to climb the ladder of success.

Commit to be a ladder-holder so that people around you can become successful in their lives. In doing so, you will live a content and extremely successful life.

#67

Download the new Communist Texting Filter App-
you type your text, then the app changes anything that
may be construed as anti-communist. Basically, it
changes everything but your name. Names are not
changed to protect the innocent.

Send a text to someone that has truly impacted your
life. Freely tell them how much you have benefited
from their influence. Don't hold back, no one is going
to modify your text.

#68

Drives that momentarily take your breath away are great, but drives that permanently take your breath away are not.

Take a scenic drive and enjoy the beauty of creation. Make sure you keep at least one eye on the road.

#69

Whispering – What you do when you want one person to hear.

Yelling – What you do when you want everyone to hear.

Shut your mouth – What you do when *you* want to hear.

Practice the art of listening.

Know this, my beloved brothers: Let every person be quick to hear, slow to speak, slow to anger: for the anger of man does not produce the righteousness of God.

James 1:19, 20

#70

Some people have a great fear of public speaking. For people with multiple personalities, talking to themselves is public speaking.

Find ways to overcome your fear of public speaking. You can start by speaking to a group of two people. You have good things to say that others need to hear.

#71

Cats bury their poop, and dogs don't. Through this practice, cats convince people to faithfully serve them, fooling humans into believing they don't have to take crap from their cats.

Go on a trip to the zoo with your friends to watch the big cats. While there, find out practical ways you can serve your friends in the upcoming weeks. A life of service to others is a life well lived.

#72

A person's life can be like a train. You start slow, gain momentum, and begin to reach a high rate of speed, but, if you start to blow smoke about your accomplishments and toot your own whistle, you will later get derailed by pride.

Take a train trip to a nearby city, and enjoy the sights that you otherwise would not see from the highway. As you journey, make a life-long commitment to have a modest view of yourself. Live a humble life and stay on track.

One's pride will bring him low, but he who is lowly in spirit will obtain honor.

Proverbs 29:23

#73

Anonymous is a great name for parents to choose for their child. It promotes humility—they can do great things and remain anonymous.

Do an anonymous act of kindness. Leave a gift at someone's door without your name on it (unless your name is Anonymous). Pay for someone's coffee or meal without them knowing who did it. Use your imagination.

#74

Think of one thing about yourself that no one else knows, not even yourself.

Ask one of your friends questions about themselves to find out something you didn't know about them.

#75

Airports have skycaps and windsocks—why don't they also have airshoes and cloudshirts?

Next time you are traveling by airplane, go to an airport coffee shop, buy a cup of coffee, sit at a table near the cash register, and watch people. For some people traveling on a plane is stressful. When you see someone in the coffee line that looks stressed out, go to the register and pay for their coffee. It's a small price to pay to make their travels better.

#76

In baseball, a no-hitter is a great accomplishment, but in bowling it's nothing to brag about.

Take some young people to the bowling alley, pay for their game, and mentor them. The good counsel you give them could prevent them from winding up in the moral gutter.

#77

Children look forward to when the circus comes to town. In a place that is inhabited only by clowns, what do their children look forward to seeing come to town?

Take your children to the circus and clown around with them. If you don't have children, volunteer to take your relative's children to the circus.

#78

Famous last words of an artist to a gunfighter: "I can draw faster than you."

Spend some time drawing pictures with your friends. It could be a time filled with laughter and interesting conversation.

#79

Ghost towns are the place where ghostwriters go to live when they retire.

Go and visit an old west ghost town. Try and imagine what it must have been like to live there. Be thankful that you have electricity, running water, and all the modern conveniences.

#80

Valleys are mountains that are upside down.

Hike up a mountain with friends, and take in all the beautiful sights of creation that lie below you.

#81

A town tried to save money by buying incomplete traffic lights that only contained a red light. They did save money on the traffic lights, but they spent a fortune on signs that said, *No Parking*.

Next time you go to the store, park in a spot that is far from the front door. This will allow someone else to park closer to the entrance, and it will give you extra exercise.

#82

Death is the period at the end of the sentence written about your life on earth.

Our lives on earth are short. Your earthly life is limited, therefore, use it wisely.

Man is like a breath; his days are like a passing shadow.

Psalm 144:4

#83

Some individuals are magnetically drawn toward people in uniform. If you don't believe that, just ask dogs how they feel about people in postal uniforms.

Honor someone who wore a uniform in service to their country.

#84

Cliff dwellings were some of the earliest high-rise apartment buildings.

Take a trip to see and explore Native American cliff dwellings. Make sure you check out the penthouse apartment.

#85

In English, the word *red* contains fewer letters than the word for any other color. Sometimes, though, you may read that red has four letters. I don't know if you have read that before or not.

Read a biography about a person who has done great things with their life. It's okay if the book doesn't have a red cover.

#86

Fences are built to keep some things out, and some things in. Hate is a fence that keeps people on the outside of your life, and fences you in with isolation.

Open the gate in the fence you have built around yourself. Go visit with someone you don't like. You may discover things you enjoy about them.

#87

If you're good with your hands, you're called handy. If you're good with your brain, you're called brainy. Unfortunately, being called "nosy" doesn't mean you are good with your nose.

Respect and love your neighbors. Don't stick your nose into their business. If you know the happenings going on in their family, don't gossip. Stay out of trouble, and try to keep your nose clean.

#88

Unlike in former centuries, a lot of people today have x-ray vision. They belong to a group called x-ray techs, also known as radiologic technologists.

Next time you have a doctor's visit or must go to the hospital, tell the medical staff thanks for helping you to be healthy. These medical superheroes work long hours to ensure their patient's well-being. Be genuine with your thanks—if you're not, they will probably be able to see right through your insincerity.

#89

We use names of sweet foods as nicknames for our spouses, or significant others. Names like *honey*, *cookie*, *sugar*, *muffin*, or *cupcake* are often used to express love and affection. I don't think *sour cream* will ever make this list.

Tell your special someone what you appreciate about them. After telling them how much you love them, go out for a sweet treat.

#90

We call people we love *sugar*, but no one calls their loved one's *aspartame*, *sucralose*, or *saccharin*. No one uses the names of man-made sweeteners as terms of endearment—it's just not natural.

Be more aware of what you are putting into your body. Do it out of love for yourself, and for your loved ones.

#91

A fence is a person who buys stolen goods. A fence is also something you build around your property to keep people from stealing your goods.

Tell a police officer you appreciate their work in making your neighborhood safer.

#92

A hole-in-one is great, except when you're talking about your automobile tire.

Drive to the driving range, and drive some golf balls far away from you. This will help to drive the frustration of flat tires and other difficulties you've had on the road of life out of your mind for a little while. Don't give up, just keep rolling.

#93

People who mow artificial grass have a terribly boring job. They spend their entire career waiting for something to do.

Stop saying, "I'm bored." Go outside and do something. There are always things to do. If you don't have anyone to do something with, then just ask an artificial grass-mower to go with you. They're always looking for something to do.

#94

A fist-bump to the fist is good. Fist-bump to the face—not so good.

Congratulate and celebrate with the people around you who accomplish great things, win awards, or see their dreams come true. Give them a congratulatory fist-bump and say, "Well done!" If you are envious of others, their success will be like a fist-bump to your face.

#95

Why do we say *uncle* when we give up? It's all relative, for we have all had various types of relatives who have quit at one time or the other.

As you pursue your goals, don't give up despite difficulties or obstacles that may come your way. When accomplishing your dreams becomes tough, don't say, *relative*, and give up.

#96

Construction workers put up signs that say, *Men at Work*, so drivers will know they're doing something. Everyone who is working should put up a sign that reads, *Man at Work*, or, *Woman at Work*, so their bosses won't ask them if they're doing their job.

Work hard and be a good worker. Doing a great job at your work will bring you satisfaction, and it will make your boss's job easier.

#97

A rooster crows very early in the morning to remind you to turn your alarm clock off before it sounds and wakes up the rest of the household.

Wake up early, and spend some time in contemplation and prayer with God before the rest of the household wakes up. If you get up before your alarm goes off, make sure you disengage it. This act of thoughtfulness toward those in your house who are still asleep will make roosters proud.

"Be still, and know that I am God. I will be exalted among the nations, I will be exalted in the earth!"

Psalm 46:10

#98

The Multiple Personalities Anonymous group didn't last long. I'm not naming any names, but the personalities that didn't want to be healed found out about the meetings, protested, and refused to remain anonymous.

We all have different backgrounds, abilities, personalities, experiences and training. Sit and talk with someone who is very different from you. Your life will be enriched by learning about others.

#99

Some people are taken to the police station for free. I know this is true, because when people are released from the police station, I've heard them say, "I wasn't charged."

Do some work to help someone, and don't charge them for your labor. In doing so, you will be paid back with good feelings in your heart.

#100

A selfie is a photograph you take of yourself. A snapshot is an informal photograph taken by your friend or companion. A mugshot is a photograph of your face taken by the police. If most of your photos are selfies, then you need more friends. If most of your photos are mugshots, then you have a different problem. You may need to get rid of your friends.

Make a new friend, and celebrate the new friendship by taking a photograph together.

#101

I don't know why the butcher's shop didn't do well in the vegetarian community even though all the beef he sold was grain-fed.

Make a large salad with a plentiful variety of vegetables, and ask your friends over for dinner. The cows send their thanks for eating greens like they do.

#102

Littering is illegal in every city, but if you disguise your trash as confetti, you can litter legally every time there is a large celebration.

Volunteer to help clean-up after your city or town has a major celebration event.

#103

People say they are in the *doghouse* when someone is upset with them for something they did, or did not do. Does that mean that dogs who live in a doghouse are always in trouble?

Apologize to someone you have hurt. Tell them you are sorry for what you said, or did. Difficulties will come to our relationships, but when we work through them together, it gives us stronger bonds.

#104

Take Your Pet to Work Day was a smashing success, until Bob's ant tried to dance with Suzie's elephant at the after-work dance party.

Get together with your co-workers at the park to walk your dogs. This will provide a relaxing environment to build stronger relationships with them.

#105

It's better to receive a head shot from a camera than from a gun.

If you don't have a passport, go and have a passport photo taken and apply for one. Once you receive your passport in the mail, you are ready to shoot off to another country. Make sure you take your camera so you can get some good shots.

#106

Governments are obsessed with ensuring that their citizens have good health and fitness. That is why each government has a national agency solely dedicated to deal with people who say they are genuinely physically fit, but are not. It is called Central Counterfeit Agency.

Get together with a friend to work out on a regular basis. Don't have counterfeit fitness, but work toward being genuinely fit.

#107

Psychology experts say that each person needs several human touches a day to have good emotional health. That's why a boxer feels so loved. A boxer receives hundreds of human touches a day—most of them in the form of punches to the face.

Give a friend a hug, and encourage them. Your hug will touch their heart.

#108

Naps are your body telling you that you failed during last night's sleep. Nags are people telling you that you failed to do something they wanted done, and they will not let you sleep until it is completed.

Make sure you get a sufficient amount of sleep each night. If you don't, you might get cranky and start to nag people. Sufficient sleep, a healthy diet, and regular exercise are very important for our health.

#109

Membership cards show that a person is a member of a club or organization. Shouldn't non-members also have cards to show that they are not members? That way they could be an official non-member card holder.

Join a club or organization that is doing good works to make your community a better place to live. If you want to be adventurous, you and your friends can start your own club. If you do start your own club, have fun designing your membership cards!

#110

Teachers tell their students they should be like sponges. Does that mean they should be soggy, smelly, and sit next to the sink?

Start a book club with your friends. Meet once a week to discuss a book, have some snacks and a few laughs. Practice improving your reading retention, and, bring a large sponge to the meeting just in case someone spills their beverage.

#111

The root word *nesia* comes from the Greek language and means *islands*. Therefore, *Micronesia* means small islands, *Polynesia* means many islands, and *Indonesia* means Indian islands. It makes perfect sense that *amnesia* means that I can't remember what island I am from.

Plan a trip to an island. Spend half of each day you are there helping some charity organization, and the other half relaxing or sight-seeing.

#112

The pastor of a cult was asked to resign for promoting false teaching.

Always pursue, follow, and speak the truth. Jesus said,

"If you abide in my word, you are truly my disciples, and you will know the truth, and the truth will set you free."

John 8:31, 32

#113

An example of a blanket statement: "I love all the blankets in the world."

Buy a blanket and give it to a homeless person or a poor family. You may not be able to give a blanket to all the people in the world who are cold, but you can make one person feel warm.

#114

The sound of running water is peaceful and soothing-except when it is spilling onto your kitchen floor from under your sink.

Go to a river or park water fountain. Listen to the running water; relax, breathe deeply and think about changes and decisions you need to make.

#115

There was a taxidermist who specialized in stuffing microscopic organisms. His work went practically unnoticed until the invention of the microscope.

Tell someone at work that is doing a good job that you noticed their diligent labor, and admire their work ethic. Help your co-workers to feel that their work is not microscopic.

#116

Airlines have safety information brochures in the seat pocket in front of you, telling you what to do in case of an emergency landing. Shouldn't the airlines be more positive, and tell you what to do in case of a safe landing?

Be positive, and encourage people to continue to do the good things you see them doing. This encouragement will help them to soar to new heights.

#117

When you are late for your appointments you are stealing grains of sand out of other's hour-glasses.

People only have so many hours each day in their time accounts, so don't be late for your appointments, and rob them of their minutes. Stealing is wrong. Work hard to be early, or at least be on time. Cease your chronic criminal activity of tardiness.

#118

"I ate nothing tomorrow."

Tomorrow never comes. When the day after today arrives, it will be today. Make today a monumental day. What will you eat and do today? Who will you spend time with today? Make a difference today—don't wait until tomorrow.

#119

Common ancient saying spoken to Dragon Slayers:
"Only *you* can prevent dragon fires."

When you go camping, leave the land the way you found it. Make sure you pick up your trash, and completely extinguish your campfire. Ensure that your family, and others have a beautiful place to go camping in the future.

#120

A mannequin really has only two major career options. One as a clothing model, the second as a crash dummy. In the first career option the mannequin stands in a store window. In the second it goes through a car window. When a mannequin gets a job as a crash dummy, it knows its career is out the window.

Help someone who is unemployed find a job. Remember that job hunting and window shopping are similar; you look a lot of places before any money is exchanged. Don't give up—your dream job is waiting for you in reality.

#121

If you have trouble smiling, stand on your head and turn your frown upside-down.

Give people a smile! Exercising daily smiles will build up your smiling muscles, and will encourage others to do smile work-outs. Smile. You're burning calories. :)

#122

Flight attendants are truly brave and talented people, serving snacks and beverages to ungrateful passengers while walking on a narrow walkway, eight miles in the air, without a net.

Next time you travel, try not to be a demanding customer. Make the workers feel glad that you visited their work place on your vacation.

#123

My family said they were going to shower me with gifts. "Shower me with gifts" meant that I got a shower head as a gift, and they wanted me to install it.

Shower those around you with love and kindness. No one will complain about the cascading compassion, or flowing friendliness.

#124

Job Catch phrases of Hippies

Ditch Digger – "I'm diggin' it man!"

Concrete Worker – "That's solid man!"

Rocketeer – "Out of sight dude!"

Block Ice Maker – "That's cool man!"

Rancher – "Dude!"

Botanist – "Flower Power!"

Carpenter – "Nailed it dude!"

Air Conditioner Repairman – "No sweat man!"

Hip Replacement Specialist – "That's hip, man!"

Take pride in your work. If you don't like your job, consider a career change. Doing a job you love for less pay is better than being paid more to do a job you hate. Can you dig what I'm sayin' man?

#125

Why do they call it a park if I have to keep my car outside?

Take a walk in the park to enjoy the flowers, trees, and lush grass. Walking is great exercise, and also the earliest known form of transportation.

#126

Moms sometimes tell their children to finish everything on their plate even when the child is full, because there are starving children around the world. I don't understand how promoting obesity will help starving children.

Donate to help those who are hungry. Deposit food in a food bank so starving people can make a withdrawal. Fighting world hunger starts in your own neighborhood.

Whoever despises his neighbor is a sinner, but blessed is he who is generous to the poor.

Proverbs 14:21

#127

When something is neither cold nor hot we call it luke-warm. Why don't other temperatures also have names, like Phil-cold, or Barry-hot?

Be thankful for whatever weather you are given today, whether you like it or not. At least you are alive, and healthy enough to go outside into the weather. Some people are confined to their bed, and are unable to go outdoors. Thank God I can go outside and stand in the rain.

#128

There is a new phone calculator app for people who like to count on their fingers. If you type 2 x 4 into the app, it converts it to 2 fingers x 4 fingers = 8 fingers. This app is very useful when you are counting higher than ten.

Count on your fingers those who are your good friends. They are the ones you can always count on to be there for you. Send them a greeting card and express how grateful you are for their friendship.

#129

A work office has lots of paperwork to do. An office restroom is no exception to this truth. Both require finishing the paperwork before you can leave.

Write a letter to your spouse or significant other, and tell them how much you love and appreciate them. Mail it to them. Everyone loves receiving personal letters in the mail.

#130

A desert is miles of beach without an ocean, or hordes of sunbathers.

Go to the desert and enjoy the uncrowded space and peaceful surroundings. A deserted desert is an ideal place to sit, and reflect on your life. If you choose to, bring a towel and sunbathe as the waves of heat splash over you.

About the Author

Rodney Charles Dutton grew up in southern Oklahoma. He has lived in every time zone of the lower forty-eight states of the U.S.A. He has also visited twenty-six countries and had the privilege of living in India for three years. Rodney loves learning about history, cultures and languages. Diversity intrigues him and he feels comfortable in multicultural settings. Photography fascinates him. Creating and sharing his short stories, children's stories and poetry give him great joy. Rodney currently lives in New Mexico. You can contact the author at **RodneyCharlesDutton@yahoo.com**

Books by Rodney Charles Dutton

Above, Beside, Below: Poetry by Rodney Charles Dutton

Look At That! The Life of Francine the Watchful Cat (Children's Storybook)

Look At That! The Life of Francine the Watchful Cat (Children's Companion Activity Book)